THE SECRET OF
UNLIMITED PROSPERITY

THE
SECRET OF
UNLIMITED
PROSPERITY

Catherine Ponder

DeVorss Publications
Camarillo, California

The Secret of Unlimited Prosperity
Copyright © 1981 by Catherine Ponder

ISBN: 978-087516-419-9

DeVorss & Company, Publisher
PO Box 1389
Camarillo CA 93011-1389
www.devorss.com

Printed in the United States of America

CONTENTS

1. THE SECRET OF UNLIMITED

How to open your mind to unlimited supply. The source
of your supply. Your supply can come in many ways.
Share your supply. What sharing through systematic
giving can do for you. Sharing with God pays debts.
Why you can't afford not to tithe. How tithing releases
unlimited supply.

2. THE PROSPERITY LAW OF RECEIVING

You always have something to give. Expect to receive.
The great law of "give and take." Giving multiplies

your returns. Open the channels to your good. The law of receiving. Stolen good restored. Protection through giving. From bankruptcy to stable prosperity. Give, then expect to receive. Expect more! Become permanently prosperous.

3. THE PROSPERITY LAW OF MENTAL

What you think, you attract. Business and the law of attraction. Joshua's use of the law of attraction. Secret thoughts attract. The attracting power of hatred. Your thoughts make your world. Fear can keep away our good. Picture the best. Like attracts like.

4. THE PROSPERITY LAW OF MENTAL

Mental acceptance and the Promised Land. Why some demonstrate Truth and others do not. The formula for accepting your good: Release the past. Think of your life as you want it to be. Get ready to accept your good.

Introduction:

AN ANCIENT PROSPERITY

FORMULA FOR YOU!

A Special Message From The Author

In these pages, I am happy to share with you an ancient prosperity formula! I first taught this simple formula to a group of business people in 1958 to help them go *from recession to abundance.*

The results of that class were so successful that they led to the writing of my first book, *The Dynamic Laws of Prosperity.* A dozen books have followed, including my popular new series on "The Millionaires of the Bible." I have been thrilled—as have been my readers—to learn that the Biblical millionaires used this mystic success formula too.

Hundreds of thousands of my readers have applied this age-old formula during the past twenty years, and their reports to me indicate that they have experienced countless benefits. A reader in New Mexico wrote:

> I first heard you describe this ancient prosperity formula when you spoke in Albuquerque in 1969. I don't know why it took me so long to "let it happen." But when I finally began using this method, *my life changed for the good so rapidly and so completely that I could hardly believe it.*
>
> Now for the first time, I love and appreciate *me*, as well as understanding God as a loving Father. The use of this prosperity formula has brought a greater love toward and from my family and friends. I have applied this success formula toward those with whom I work with appreciative results too.
>
> Catherine, I truly believe *The Secret of Unlimited Prosperity* is *the finest pocket guide to successful living I have ever read!* I shall be sending copies to all my loved ones and friends, both near and far.

My personal use of this formula has gradually helped me to grow over a period of years from a one-room existence in Alabama to a pleasant life style in the famous Palm Springs-Palm Desert area of Southern California.

This formula has also helped me to found three churches from "financial scratch" over the years — at a time when many traditionally-funded churches have suffered from financial strain because of our changing economic times. I am now blessed — for the first time — with adequate staff, equipment and facilities to carry on my ever-expanding global ministry.

As you study and apply the simple prosperity formula described herein, I invite you to write me of your happy results, so that I may share them with my readers everywhere.

Meanwhile, I shall be declaring "ABUNDANT EXPERIENCES IN UNLIMITED PROSPERITY" for you and yours! Together, let us prove anew this ancient formula for successful living.

Catherine Ponder

P.O. Drawer 1278
Palm Desert, California, 92261
U.S.A.

THE SECRET OF UNLIMITED PROSPERITY

— Chapter 1 —

A housewife was trying to demonstrate greater prosperity for her family. She said: "I have it all figured out. We need additional money to meet unexpected expenses that have arisen. We are on a 'fixed income.' Our only channel of supply is my husband's salary. I have been praying for and affirming increased prosperity. Why doesn't my husband's employer cooperate by giving him a raise?" She had not yet learned the secret of unlimited prosperity.

Many people cut off the flow of substance because they think of substance as fixed in form. Never say that you are on a "fixed income."

The very statement closes your mind and your pocketbook to new channels of supply that are constantly trying to open to you.

Charles Fillmore has explained in his book *Prosperity:*[1]

> We must not try to fix the avenues through which our good is to come. . . . Trying to fix the channel through which his good must come to him is one of the ways in which the personal man shuts off his own supply.

The basic secret of unlimited prosperity is this: God is the source of man's supply, and He has provided many channels through which the riches of the universe can flow to him. Moses reminded the Hebrews of this secret when he said,"You shall remember the Lord your God, for it is he who gives you power to get wealth." (Deuteronomy 8:18)

HOW TO OPEN YOUR MIND TO UNLIMITED SUPPLY

Begin now to open your mind to the unlimited supply of the universe that is yours by divine right

1. Charles Fillmore, *Prosperity* (Unity Village, Mo: Unity Books, 1936).

by affirming often: "*I do not depend on persons or conditions for my supply. God is the source of my supply, and He is constantly opening new channels of prosperity to me. I am open and receptive to my highest good now.*" Then watch the ideas, opportunities, and events that come. They will be the keys to your unlimited supply.

In her book *What Are You?*[2] Imelda Shanklin explains further the secret of unlimited prosperity:

> There is no numbering of the avenues through which supply may come to you. . . . Your resource is as far-reaching as the universe. . . . You are to expect your supply through all avenues of contact with life. Not from one specified point, not from two or more specified points; but from all points of the universe your good is crowding toward you.

The aforementioned housewife talked with a friend about her financial plight. The friend suggested she begin opening her mind to the possibility of unlimited supply by affirming: "*There is no numbering of the avenues through which supply can come to us. Our resource is as far-reaching as the universe. We expect our*

---

2. Imelda Shanklin, *What Are You?*
(Unity Village, Mo: Unity Books, 1929).

supply through all avenues of life. From all points of the universe, unlimited supply is crowding upon us now!"

As she began making these affirmations, an interesting thing happened: Near the new home she and her husband had recently moved into, the state highway department was building a new road. High-powered explosives had been used to cut through a rocky area for the right-of-way of this highway.

Some of the residents of this area had filed complaints with the highway department stating that as a result of the use of the explosives, their homes had been damaged. The highway department sent appraisers to inspect the damage and settle claims. This woman and her husband had not made any claims for damage. Nevertheless, when the officials from the highway department arrived, they insisted upon inspecting every house in the locality. In this couple's home, the appraisers detected various cracks in the walls and other defects which they felt might have resulted from the use of the explosives. They insisted upon making a settlement of $400 — which was the exact amount needed to meet the additional expenses which had arisen earlier! As this housewife continued to affirm unlimited supply, her husband later received a raise in pay, and other helpful financial demonstrations came to them.

Do not cut off the flow of substance in your life by thinking that it has to come in a certain way through certain stipulated channels. "There is no numbering of the avenues through which supply may come to you."[3] Expect your supply from all avenues of life. As you do, you will find it crowding upon you in new and different ways.

THE SOURCE OF YOUR SUPPLY

A West Coast stockbroker was trying to support his family on an annual income of $7,200. It was a struggle. Then he purchased a copy of Charles Fillmore's book, *Prosperity.* From this book, he learned the secret of unlimited prosperity: God was the source of his supply; substance is the body of God and has been given man for his unlimited good; thought is the master of substance, and by deliberately directing his thoughts toward prosperity, his thoughts would move on the rich substance of the universe and produce prosperous results for him. He began affirming: *"Father, I thank Thee for*

---

3. Ibid.

unlimited increase in mind, money, and affairs."
Within one year, his income had zoomed upward
from $7,200 to $40,000!

As Imelda Shanklin has written:[4]

> Substance is your resource, your support. It
> is your bodily support; it is your financial sup-
> port. . . . Intelligent contact with substance is
> your most pertinent need in the visible world.

YOUR SUPPLY CAN COME IN MANY WAYS

A Protestant minister had been struggling to
support his family on an annual income of
$6,000. It was a frustrating experience. As he
prayed for guidance, a friend introduced him to
some Truth teachings on prosperity which he
found especially helpful.

He, too, learned the secret of unlimited prosperity: that his financial income was not fixed
of form, but could come to him in countless
ways. As he began to realize this, an unforseen
thing happened:

He had been serving as a fund-raiser for his
denomination. Whenever a new church was
needed in a community, he would visit the con-
gregation, and arrange for the purchase of

---

4. Ibid.

church bonds to finance the building of the church. He had never been paid for his services, although through his hard work several million dollars had been raised, and a number of churches had been built.

As he began affirming that all financial doors were open to him, that all financial channels were free, and that unlimited supply was his by divine right, he was informed by the officials of his denomination that he would begin receiving a percentage of the money that was raised for new church building (just as had the professional money-raising organizations which had previously worked for this denomination, with much less success than this minister).

Thus this man's income went from $6,000 to $30,000 the year after he began affirming unlimited supply. Like Job, he had learned the meaning of the wonderful promise:" . . . the Almighty is your gold, and your precious silver." (Job 22:25)

You will begin to understand the secret of unlimited prosperity when you realize that your supply is not fixed in form. **Your supply can come to you through expected channels, in expected ways, and it should. But your supply can also come to you through unexpected channels, in unexpected ways. From all points of the universe, your good is constantly crowd-**

ing upon you! When you dare to realize this and accept this idea, unlimited supply will find its way to you.

A statement I have used for years is: *"I give thanks that the universal spirit of prosperity is providing richly for me now."* This always seems to open new channels of supply from near and far.

SHARE YOUR SUPPLY

Along with realizing that God is the source of your supply; that He has unlimited channels, both near and far, through which your supply can manifest; that He has provided unlimited substance for your provision; that your supply is, therefore, not fixed in form, but can come to you from all points of the universe—there is yet another aspect of the secret of unlimited supply to consider:

You must share your supply if you would insure continuation of your supply. In practical ways, you will find that sharing and expectancy are the beginning of financial increase.

Most people who think they are on a limited income feel they cannot afford to share or give. By not giving, they stop their own receiving of greater supply, because they are violating the universal law of prosperity. They have not yet learned the secret of unlimited supply pointed out by Solomon:

"One man gives freely, yet grows all the
          richer;
     another withholds what he should give,
          and only suffers want.
A liberal man will be enriched,
     and one who waters will himself be
          watered."

(Proverbs 11:24,25)

WHAT SHARING THROUGH SYSTEMATIC GIVING CAN DO FOR YOU

One of the most scientific, businesslike, and spiritual ways of sharing is through the act of tithing one-tenth of one's gross income to God's work. Systematic giving opens the way to systematic receiving.

When you think you cannot afford to give is the very time when you cannot afford *not* to give! If through your own wisdom you have been unable to realize unlimited supply, then you need divine wisdom to guide you into greater abundance. You are the rich child of a loving Father; by putting God first financially, you make contact with His wisdom, and with His unlimited bounty which has been provided for you.

A woman was in dire need of several hundred dollars to pay pressing debts. She realized that she must give if she wished to receive. She wrote out a check for the balance in her account. This check represented a tithe offering of the money she wished to demonstrate to pay her bills. Upon giving this tithe check to a local church she said to the minister: "Here is my advance tithe offering from the money I expect to demonstrate. I am going to demonstrate or starve, but I know I shall demonstrate, because I am giving, thereby invoking the prosperity law." Shortly, from a totally unexpected channel, she received a check for $400 and was able to pay every bill. But nothing happened—the prosperity demonstration did not come—until she first gave.

It is true: you must share your substance to insure continuation of your substance. Sharing and expectancy are the beginning of financial increase. The marvelous truth is that when you give or share, you automatically begin to expect fresh new supply to come to you, because you know you have invoked the prosperity law fully. Your faith and expectancy open the way.

A man who has tithed since childhood firmly believes that when a person is in financial difficulties, the best way to get out of them is to tithe. The Scriptures reveal that while the ancient Hebrews tithed to their priests and places of worship, they prospered. But when they wandered away from the Lord in the matter of tithing, hardships came upon them.

SHARING WITH GOD PAYS DEBTS

A couple had struggled long and hard to realize greater prosperity in order to pay off financial obligations. In spite of hard work and stringent budgeting (which had only added to the thought of lack), things had grown steadily worse. One day they heard a lecture on the wisdom of tithing one's way to prosperity.

In desperation they decided to try it, reasoning that the amount of their tithe could not go far toward paying their debts, so they would hardly miss it anyway. As they began to tithe a tenth of their income to God's work, they began to feel peaceful and secure, rather than tense, about their financial affairs. As they continued to share their substance with God, certain property that they owned was sold at a good price for a business development. From the proceeds of this sale, they were able to pay every debt. Sharing and expectancy proved to be the beginning of their financial increase. As they continued to tithe, their joint incomes increased, their money seemed to go further, and they were freed of all financial strain.

Tithing establishes order in mind, body, and affairs. When order exists, one cannot remain in debt.

WHY YOU CAN'T AFFORD NOT TO TITHE

A professional man in retirement was in dire circumstances, having lost his life savings in some unwise financial ventures. His only income was a pension of about eighty dollars per month. When he told a friend of his financial plight, the friend suggested that he begin to tithe his way to unlimited prosperity. He replied indignantly, "I can't afford to tithe!" The friend reminded him: "You can't afford *not* to tithe. In your financial circumstances, you have no choice but to trust God completely. And if you can't trust God to guide you financially, whom can you trust? Who has greater wisdom? Who is richer? Who wants you to be prosperous, more than your loving Father? Who is better equipped to help you than He is?"

Realizing the logic of this, the retired man agreed to begin tithing $8 from his pension check each month. As he did, an almost unbelievable thing happened. For some time he had had an interesting theory about certain stock market investments, and had worked out a chart based on his theory. Though previously no one had seemed interested in his ideas, simultaneously several prosperous investors asked him to use his theory on certain of their stocks. He did, and they were prospered. He soon reported to his friend who had suggested that he tithe, "This week alone I made $800 helping those investors with certain of their stocks." The friend gently reminded him that $800 a week was a far better income than $80 a month, and that he had surely proved it pays to put God first financially through tithing.

HOW TITHING RELEASES
UNLIMITED SUPPLY

Charles Fillmore has explained why the act of tithing releases unlimited supply:[5]

When a person tithes he is giving continuously, so that no spirit of grasping, no fear, and

5. Fillmore, *Prosperity*.

no thought of limitation gets a hold upon him. There is nothing that keeps a person's mind so fearless and so free to receive the good constantly coming to him as the practice of tithing. . . . Tithing is based upon a law that cannot fail, and it is the surest way ever found to demonstrate plenty, for it is God's own law and way of giving.

For your own ventures in realizing unlimited supply, you will want to affirm:

"I will remember Jehovah God, for He it is that gives me power to experience wealth. I give richly and I receive richly now. I tithe my way to unlimited prosperity now."

A SPECIAL NOTE FROM THE AUTHOR

Through the generous outpouring of their tithes over the years, the readers of my books have helped me to financially establish three new churches—the most recent being a global ministry, the nondenominational *Unity Church Worldwide*, with headquarters in Palm Desert, California. Many thanks for your help in the past, and for all that you continue to share.

You are also invited to share your tithes with the churches of your choice—especially those which teach the truths stressed in this book. Such churches would include the metaphysical churches of Unity, Religious Science, Divine Science, Science of Mind, Centers for Spiritual Living, and other related churches, many of which are members of The International New Thought Movement. For a list of such churches write The International New Thought Alliance, 5003 E. Broadway Rd., Mesa AZ 85206, or visit their website:www.newthoughtalliance.org. Your support of such churches can help spread the prosperous Truth that mankind is now seeking in this New Age of metaphysical enlightenment.

THE PROSPERITY LAW OF RECEIVING

— Chapter 2 —

The first step in receiving is giving. It is through the law of giving and receiving that we demonstrate prosperity. If you are not receiving the good you feel you should have in life, ask yourself, "What should I give?"

In *The Revealing Word,*[1] Charles Fillmore has explained: "It is necessary to give freely if we are to receive freely. The law of receiving includes giving."

Prosperity is omnipresent, and you cannot impoverish yourself by giving. Instead you are

---

1. Unity Books, (Unity Village, Mo., 64065, 1959).

enriched by giving, which opens the way for you to receive.

YOU ALWAYS HAVE SOMETHING TO GIVE

Since prosperity is omnipresent, you always have something to give! A widow with a houseful of small children telephoned a Unity counselor. She had no money or food for her children. It was lunch time and her children had not eaten since the day before. She desperately needed to demonstrate prosperity.

The counselor knew that giving is the first step in receiving; that one is never impoverished by giving, but is enriched. She explained that the widow must first *give* in some way; that the act of giving would move on universal substance, and would start substance flowing back to her in some appropriate form.

The widow's first reaction was much the same as yours or mine may have been the first time we were told we must give in order to receive. She lamented: "But that's just the problem! I have nothing to give." To which the counselor replied: "Of course you have something to give. *We always have something to give.*" The counselor then urged this frantic widow to look about her and ask for divine guidance concerning what she could give.

It was further suggested that, after starting the flow of substance by giving, she should get ready to receive by preparing her table for the meal she wanted for her children; and by preparing her grocery list for shopping, in the assurance that the necessary money would appear very soon.

Hesitantly the widow followed instructions. Suddenly she remembered flowers growing in her yard; she cut them and gave them to a sick neighbor, who seemed overjoyed to receive them. Next she prepared her table with the best china, silver, and linens in the house. This gave the children pleasure and excitement, and they expectantly awaited a good meal. Just as she was completing her grocery list, someone who had owed her money for a long time dropped by and paid her $30 on the debt. Thus she proved that giving is the first step in receiving.

EXPECT TO RECEIVE

We have all heard about the law of compensation: we cannot get something for nothing; we must give in order to receive. But often we have tried to bypass this basic law of prosperity; and in attempting to make short cuts, we have only bypassed our good.

The formula is simple: If you are not receiving the good you want in life, ask yourself, "What can I give, to make way to receive my good?" Then freely and quickly give it! There are those pious souls who will say, "Oh, but when I give, I am not supposed to expect to receive." And so, of course, they do not receive. Their very attitude blocks their good.

Quite the opposite is true: When you give, you can and should expect to receive. It is the law of the universe. Jesus pointed out the great law of receiving when He promised: "Give, and it will be given to you; good measure, pressed down, shaken together, running over, will they put into your lap. For the measure you give will be the measure you get back." (Luke 6:38)

THE GREAT LAW OF "GIVE AND TAKE"

Someone has called it "the great law of give and take." Give, and then you can take or claim your own abundance from the rich universe, because through your act of giving you have opened the channel through which universal supply can pour forth to you in appropriate form.

A real-estate man in Palm Beach, Florida, had an apartment which had not rented for "the season," though it was ideally located halfway between the beach fronting the Atlantic Ocean and Lake Worth. He had made every effort (from a business standpoint) to rent it. When he heard a prosperity lecture on "the great law of give and take," he realized that he needed to give something away, in order to make way to claim his prosperity from the rental of the apartment.

As he was asking, "What can I give?" he received word from out-of-town friends that they were coming to Palm Beach for a month's vacation. They asked him to recommend a place where they could stay. This was the answer to his desire to give: he made them a gift of the unrented apartment for their month's stay. During that month, he succeeded in renting the apartment for the entire approaching "season." But nothing had happened, until he gave *first*.

GIVING MULTIPLIES YOUR RETURNS

In his book *Working with God*,[2] Gardner Hunting has described the law of giving and

---

2. Gardner Hunting, *Working with God*,
(Unity Village, Mo., Unity Books, 1934).

receiving as the law of "come-back": what you give comes back to you multiplied. He advises:

> Right where you are, now, begin to give something good to the person nearest you, and keep on doing it, no matter what you seem to get back at first. *Do!* Don't talk! And you'll lift yourself out of your troubles, no matter what they seem to be or how deeply you seem to be sunk in them. Try it. You'll be surprised. . . . Try it patiently and as hard as you would try to get a drink of water if you were very thirsty. You'll get a return, a reward, that you don't even dream of yet.
>
> Any man, woman, or child can transform his life by transforming the thing he gives out.

A friend of mine knows a businessman who began studying these ideas in *Working with God* before World War II. As he began to give out in every way that was revealed to him, he had a dream one night in which the idea for a special kind of landing gear for airplanes was revealed to him. He followed through on his dream, and invented the landing gear. It was used during the war on planes all over the world. Since that time this man has made other mechanical inventions that have helped mankind. Needless to say, he quickly became a millionaire; and he continues to give, give, give, because he realizes this to be the secret of his affluence. Among the things he has given away are hundreds of copies of inspirational books, and he has given large amounts of money, land, and other gifts to his church.

OPEN THE CHANNELS TO YOUR GOOD

Gardner Hunting has also written, "Many things you want most are now within your reach." By the act of giving, you open the way for the things within your reach to appear quickly. These things have been wanting to come to you all the time, but were blocked by your lack of giving, because there was no free channel through which they could appear. Your giving opens and frees the channel. Always when there seems to be delay, confusion, or a block between you and your good, that block lies *within* you, and not in some outside circumstance or personality. When you give under divine guidance, you dissolve the block and open a channel for your good. Then nothing can stop its manifestation in your life! (Nothing has stopped its manifestation previously but your own lack of giving.)

THE LAW OF RECEIVING

It is true that you cannot get something for nothing. You must give to make way to receive. The law also works the other way: You cannot give anything without getting something for it. Give the best you have and then look for the best in return. This is the law of receiving.

Some months ago, I received word from a friend that she wished to send me a gift. The gift she described was one of my secret heart's desires from childhood; so I gratefully accepted her offer, and awaited its arrival thankfully and expectantly.

But the gift did not arrive. For a number of weeks nothing happened. Then I mentally analyzed the situation, thinking: "If I am to receive this gift, and it has been delayed, then that delay is *within* me. I am doing something to block the receipt of this wonderful gift." In a flash I realized that I must give, to make way to receive the gift.

As I asked, "What am I supposed to give?" it suddenly dawned on me that I had a tithe gift which I had been holding, awaiting guidance about where I should give it. Since it was by far the largest tithe offering I had ever had to give, I had been hesitant to release it, wanting to be sure I gave it where it would do the most good.

With the dawning of this realization, I asked anew for guidance about the release of this offering, and gained a strong assurance that it should be given to the Unity church where I was serving. It was quickly released to the building fund.

A few days later I received in the mail the lovely gift promised me weeks earlier. The amazing thing was this: That gift had been mailed, according to its postmark, the same afternoon I finally wrote out the check for my tithe offering and released it! A little note enclosed with the gift was even greater evidence of the exactness with which the great law of giving and receiving works. The note read: "A strange thing happened. After I notified you that I was sending this gift to you, the gift disappeared! For weeks I could not find it, and felt embarrassed about its delay. After much prayer, it finally reappeared, and I am happy to send it along to you."

What my benefactor did not know was that the gift had disappeared until I had made way for it, by doing my part first, which was to give. When I realized that I must give, and did so, the gift reappeared and was quickly mailed to me. The only delay had been *within* me, through my lack of giving. When I did give, the block was dissolved. The gift promptly arrived.

STOLEN GOOD RESTORED

In the book *Effectual Prayer*,[3] Frances W. Foulks points out:

If a person would have his prayers answered he must be willing to be a channel through which the prayers of others are answered. If he would be healed he must be willing to be a healer of discords. If he would have prosperity he must be willing to become still and face the issue honestly. Admit to yourself: "Something has been taken from me, because I have not been giving as I should. I have been trying to steal my good from the universe, so now my good has been stolen from me."

Say to the supposed thief: "You did not steal from me. I give those items to you. I am the thief, not you. Thank you for bringing it to my attention." Then quietly ask what you can give, and quickly give it. As you do, you reverse the law, to make way for your good to appear. You will find that what you have lost will be divinely restored to you, if you will give and continue to give consistently.

---

3. Frances W. Foulks, *Effectual Prayer,*
(Unity Village, Mo., Unity Books, 1945).

PROTECTION THROUGH GIVING

The Bible points out clearly that when you give, you are always protected from the negative experiences of life; that it is when you are not giving that you submit yourself to the negative forces of hard times, bad crops, poor business, theft, accident, ill health, inharmony on all levels of life. Jehovah promised Abraham after he tithed, "Fear not, Abram, I am your shield; your reward shall be very great." (Genesis 15:1) Jehovah promised the Hebrews through Moses that if they kept His commandments, which included the law of tithing, they would be blessed with rain in due season; their land would yield an increase bountifully, and they would eat their bread to the full and dwell in their land safely. For these blessings Jehovah expected a tithe of their land, whether seed or fruit of the tree; a tithe of the flock, and every other possession. The tithe was considered holy unto Jehovah; it did not belong to the Hebrews. They willingly and unquestioningly gave a tenth of all their possessions and their income, and they were richly blessed.

The prophet Malachi later pointed out to the Hebrews why they had come into hard times: they were no longer tithing. "Bring the full tithes into the storehouse . . . and thereby put me to the test . . . if I will not open the windows of heaven for you and pour down for you an overflowing blessing. I will rebuke the devourer for you, so that it will not destroy the fruits of your soil; and your vine in the field shall not fail to bear, says the Lord of hosts. Then all nations will call you blessed, for you will be a land of delight." (Malachi 3:10-12)

Thus protection as well as prosperity is assured to those who recognize God as the source of their supply and keep attuned to that source, by returning to God's work at least a tenth of all He has given them. Of course, **tithing is not the only method for becoming prosperous, but tithing makes it at least ten times easier for a person to prosper, because he has invoked the highest law of prosperity and has made contact with the source of all riches, God.**

Once you have given, you should expect to receive. Open your mind to the thought of receiving. The law of receiving is this: Give, then make way to receive. Charles Fillmore has advised: "You must prepare your consciousness for the inflow of the universal substance."

FROM BANKRUPTCY TO STABLE PROSPERITY

A businessman was desperate. He had used all his capital, gained through a lifetime of hard work, to help a new company get started. The company failed, went into bankruptcy, and the man was left with more than a hundred thousand dollars worth of debts. Through sheer hard work, he reduced this indebtedness to fifty thousand dollars, though it meant great deprivation to him and his family. The financial pressure being placed upon him by his creditors was very great, until he happened to hear a lecture on the prospering power of tithing. He quickly realized that this was the only sensible way out of his predicament. He agreed with the speaker who said, "The firm of God and Man, Incorporated, never fails." This man immediately gave a tithe offering to the local Unity center. As he began to put God first financially, he felt guided and protected. The financial strain eased; his income steadily mounted. In less time than he could have dreamed possible, the indebtedness began to fade away, and he was on the road to stable prosperity.

GIVE, THEN EXPECT TO RECEIVE

I once wrote out a tithe offering for $450, which was being given to our Unity building fund. Just as I was writing out the check, my teen-age son came in, and I explained where the money was being given, saying: "We cannot give without receiving, so this money will come back to us. In fact, it will be interesting to see *how* this money will come back to us." My son casually replied, "Mother, *more* than this amount will come back to us," to which I agreed.

In a matter of days it happened. I received a gift of $750 from a friend whom I had not seen for several years. It was a gift of appreciation for some ideas that had been shared with her in a time of great need, and which had brought the desired results. My son reminded me, "There's that $450 . . . it has come back multiplied."

As you give, speak the word of receiving. Expect to receive, as you invoke the law. "Give, and it shall be given unto you."

A businesswoman gave a tithe offering of $100 to Unity School. As she gave it, she spoke the word of receiving, and shortly received an unexpected check for $99.21. A businessman gave an offering of fifteen dollars to his local Unity center. As he did, he spoke the word of receiving, and was soon informed by his bank that his savings account had just earned fifteen dollars in interest.

Another businessman gave a tithe offering to his church and spoke the word of receiving as he did so. Shortly he received a long-distance telephone call stating he would receive $3,000 in new business right away. An office worker decided to test this idea, by giving a dollar as an offering and then speaking the word of receiving. That same day she received five dollars as a gift. A student gave an offering, spoke the word of receiving, and through the mail received a gift of money from someone to whom she owed money!

EXPECT MORE!

As you give, be sure that you expect to receive at least the amount of your gift in return. However, open your mind to the thought that even more than that may come back to you. A college student gave two dollars in a church offering, expecting *more* than that amount to return to him. In a few days, he received a gift of $200 from a relative who wished to help further his education. A doctor gave an offering of a dollar, decreeing that much more would come back. He received a gift of $100 from a patient. A housewife gave an offering of $1 in anticipation of receiving much more. A customer who had owed her husband $100 (which they had previously been unable to collect) mailed a check for $100 on the very day she gave her offering.

A young man was desperate. He had traveled a long distance to take a new job, in the faith that the job was his highest good. On a day when he was down to his last fifty cents (a number of days before he would receive his first paycheck), he heard about the law of receiving. He consistently tithed, so he had already given his "all." He realized that the only block to his immediate prosperity lay in the fact that he had not opened his mind to the idea of receiving immediately. He had been limiting his prosperity by thinking that it would come only a number of days hence, as a paycheck. He began to decree: *"My prosperity is from God. My prosperity is omnipresent. I have given, through my tithes, so I have a right to receive immediate prosperity. I am receiving, I am receiving now. I am receiving all the good God has for me now!"* He made these statements of joyous expectation. The next morning he received a letter from hometown friends, expressing their delight in his new job. To show their appreciation they had enclosed a gift of twenty-five dollars.

BECOME PERMANENTLY PROSPEROUS

It is your Father's good pleasure to give you the kingdom here and now; is it your good pleasure to receive it? Begin now to invoke the law of receiving by giving, giving, giving, consistently and faithfully. Then get ready to receive. Speak the word of receiving. Prepare to receive. As you do, you can and will prove that your prosperity is omnipresent, and you will become permanently prosperous. There will be no need, in due time, for desperate on-the-spot prosperity demonstrations.

To develop a permanent prosperity consciousness, decree: *"I always have something to give and I give it. As I give consistently, I open the way to receive consistently. I give freely my tenth to God's work and workers, and I reap a hundredfold. I am receiving, I am receiving now. I am receiving all the good God has for me now. I am permanently prosperous."*

THE PROSPERITY LAW
OF MENTAL ATTRACTION

— Chapter 3 —

A professor once spoke of observing the law of attraction working among his students. Two of the classes he taught were filled with bright, well-adjusted, interested, cooperative students who came to class on time, wrote excellent themes, and were well-mannered and reasonably prosperous.

The students in his other two classes were just the opposite: They came to class late. They were unprepared, excuse-laden, uncooperative, and inattentive. Their homework was ill-prepared, and they displayed a complete lack of interest or understanding of the subject being taught. Most of them were unkempt in appearance and missed many of their class periods.

This professor remarked that the law of attraction had worked on the mental level to draw each type of student to his own group. The saying, "Birds of a feather flock together," describes the law of attraction. The students, who had been placed in groups according to an alphabetical classification only, demonstrated that law.

When we know the law we never need to go seeking — our own always comes to us. If there is one spark in you that belongs to another, you and he will meet; seas and vast continents may intervene, but by the very law of attraction you and he are bound to meet sometime.

WHAT YOU THINK, YOU ATTRACT

The law of mental attraction is one of the basic laws of the universe. We are all using it constantly, whether we are aware of it or not; in fact, we cannot help using it. The word *attract* means "to draw." You are a magnetic field of mental influence. What you think about constantly, you automatically draw, or attract to you. What you attract depends on that upon which you dwell.

You attract into your mind, body, affairs, and relationships that which you secretly harbor — what you love, and what you fear or hate. You do not so much attract what you want as what you are — according to your secret thoughts.

You attract the things to which you give a great deal of thought. If you concentrate your thoughts on injustice, you attract injustice to you. If you give a great deal of thought to lack and failure, you attract lack and failure. And you attract to you people who think the same thoughts you do.

BUSINESS AND THE LAW OF ATTRACTION

We often see the law of attraction at work in the business world as it works through ideas held in mind; ideas that create an attracting or repelling mental atmosphere. The businessman who dwells upon the goodness of God in himself and others, and who thinks about and expects success, will radiate the attracting mental atmosphere that draws success. Emerson described such a person when he said, "Great hearts send forth steadily the secret forces that incessantly draw great events."

But the businessman who dwells on limited, negative ideas, seeing only the problems and troubles of the world, holding only evil concepts of himself, his family, his business associates and the world in general, sets up a negative mental atmosphere that repels customers and success, no matter how hard he works physically.

JOSHUA'S USE OF THE LAW OF ATTRACTION

We learn a lot about the prosperity law of attraction from Joshua. It is interesting that it was Joshua who finally took the Hebrews into the Promised Land. Joshua, born in bondage, was a slave in Egypt. After he fled with the Hebrews he spent forty years with them in the wilderness. Finally Moses appointed him to take them into the Promised Land.

Joshua had worked closely with Moses in the wilderness and doubtless he learned much about the power of thought from Moses, one of the greatest metaphysicians of all times. Moses had learned the secret teachings of metaphysics during the first forty years of his life, when he was a prince in the court of Pharaoh. He had used this power throughout his life. He used it to lead the Hebrews out of bondage, to feed them in the wilderness, to lead them to the edge of the Promised Land. From Moses, Joshua also learned much about the mental law of attraction. Because of his knowledge of the law of attraction, Joshua became the logical one to lead his people into the Promised Land and to help them fully possess it.

What was the law of attraction that Joshua used to lead the Hebrews into the Promised Land? It was the same law of attraction you and I can use to take us into *our* "promised land."

From the time Joshua escaped from Egyptian bondage, he had wanted to go to the Promised Land. But many of the Hebrews could not accept the idea, even though Joshua, as a spy, had investigated it and discovered that it was a rich land, flowing with milk and honey.

The doubts of the Hebrews did not stop Joshua from dwelling in thought upon the Promised Land. He would go to the top of a high hill overlooking the Promised Land, and there he would quietly study and dwell upon it, planning how he could enter it. He worked out a plan by which he could lead the Hebrews into the land of Canaan in just three days — after a wait of forty years!

By using the law of attraction — by focusing his thoughts on the Promised Land, and on a way to enter it — Joshua invoked the law of mental attraction.[1]

1. See Catherine Ponder's books, *The Millionaire Moses* (1977), and *The Millionaire Joshua* (1978), published by DeVorss & Company, Marina del Rey, CA 90291.

SECRET THOUGHTS ATTRACT

You attract what you harbor—what you love and what you hate. Joshua harbored the idea of entering the Promised Land. He secretly loved the possibility; he thought about it; he meditated on it—and, of course, he attracted it to himself.

You can never truly evaluate another person's experiences unless you know what he is dwelling upon in thought. He may appear to be kind, positive, sincere, yet if his life does not reflect these qualities it is because he is talking one way and thinking another. "You will know them by their fruits." (Matthew 7:16) He is manifesting what he is secretly harboring in his mind, not necessarily what we would expect from the appearances he is showing to the world.

THE ATTRACTING POWER OF HATRED

A chronically unhealthy woman constantly criticized a well-known public official in her town for whom she harbored a deep hatred. One day she was informed by the local government that her home would be purchased by the city and torn down to make way for a museum that would honor the man she had hated for so many years. She had literally attracted to her that which she most resented.

Hatred is one of the strongest forms of attraction. The experience of a businesswoman who had been involved with a married man proved this. His sudden death resulted in his widow's inheriting his fortune, causing feelings of jealousy and hatred to well up in the other woman's heart.

As her hatred grew, she attracted to her innumerable problems of ill health, indebtedness, and emotional turmoil. Ironically, the hated wife began shopping in the store where the other woman worked, and seemed "drawn" to her department. The widow had known nothing of this woman's involvement with her late husband, and did not realize what emotional storms she was arousing when she approached her for advice about her purchases.

Frantically, the businesswoman asked: "Why is this happening to me? Haven't I been through enough?" Finally, she realized the irony of hate and its fantastic attracting power. It was only as she began to forgive and release the memory of past experiences and relationships that the rich widow faded out of her life. As she continued to cleanse her mind of negative emotions, she was able to resume normal living and resolve her problems.

People who constantly have negative experiences are unwittingly attracting them through their own negative thinking.

A widow of seventy-five who ran a boardinghouse hated drinking. She considered it her duty to point out to everyone she met the evils of liquor. In the process, she constantly attracted to her boardinghouse people who drank, and whom she had to evict. After this cycle had continued for some time she sought metaphysical advice and was helped to see that her own strong thoughts about drinking were the power that invariably attracted problem drinkers into her home. As she released the matter of drinking from her mind, she began to attract to her house the type of boarders she truly desired.

Health often reflects the law of attraction. A woman who repeatedly condemned her daughter-in-law complained to her friend, "Some of the things my daughter-in-law does just burn me up." Shortly after that, while preparing a meal, she burned herself severely on her hand and arm. Frantically she telephoned a Unity counselor for prayer help. The counselor said candidly: "That physical burn was attracted to you by a burning attitude. Has something or someone 'burned you up' lately?" Aghast, the woman replied weakly, "Yes, my daughter-in-law." It was only as she stopped dwelling on the actions of her daughter-in-law that the woman's health and peace of mind were restored.

YOUR THOUGHTS MAKE YOUR WORLD

Emma Curtis Hopkins has described the law of attraction: "The world in which we live is the exact record of our thoughts. If we do not like the world we live in, then we do not like our thoughts. . . . Exaltation is a magnet for all good things of the universe to hasten to you. Depression and anxiety are a magnet for trouble to fly to you."

A man whose wife had left him said: "She left me for another man. Of course, it runs in the family. My mother left my father for another man and 'lightning always strikes twice.' " He did not realize that what was "running in the family" was fear. As Job discovered long ago, the thing we fear comes upon us, because we put the law of attraction into operation.

Another man accepted the fact that: "Everyone in our family develops high blood pressure and heart trouble by the time they're sixty-two years old. They usually die by the time they're sixty-five. It runs in the family."

True to his decree, when this man reached the age of sixty-two he was told by his doctor that he had high blood pressure and heart trouble. He immediately retired from his job to await the worst. His health has steadily declined according to his expectation. He has proved the law of attraction: You attract into your body, your financial affairs, and your family relationships that which you secretly harbor — that which you love and that which you fear.

FEAR CAN KEEP AWAY OUR GOOD

Dr. Ernest C. Wilson once described the law of mental attraction:

> There is always work for the right man, and at good wages, with even bigger opportunities ready when he has proved himself capable and worthy. But even the right man is no exception to the law of right thinking.
>
> A fearful mental attitude often keeps away from us the good that God has for us. . . . A resistant mental attitude holds back the demonstration, and . . . when we dissolve the barriers of repellent thought and substitute a receptive attitude of mind, good things come to us in unexpected and wonderful ways, and sometimes with a promptness that is astonishing.

Fear and worry, the adverse mental pictures that we establish in mind, form strong barriers against the things we desire.

Is there someone you are resisting and mentally fighting? Is there some condition in mind, body, affairs, or relationships you are mentally resenting? Your resistance is holding back your good.

PICTURE THE BEST

How do you clear up mental resistance which has repelled your good? You must begin by picturing the best for yourself and for others. Stop picturing yourself as weak or misunderstood. Stop dramatizing yourself as a martyr. If you want to be thought of as long-suffering, you will always have something to suffer about. Don't take on the troubles of the world. To do so makes your life more complex and delays your good. Withdraw your strong thoughts and feelings from negation on all levels of life. Don't plan on trouble. Don't dwell on it, even if it temporarily appears. Don't even try to explain it! Let it go. Begin anew picturing the good and expecting it.

A divorced woman had long dwelt on the challenges that several unsuccessful marriages, and several problem children resulting from those marriages, had presented. For many years she had dramatized herself as a long-suffering martyr, and her problems had multiplied. Her theme song had been: "Poor, unlucky me. What a hard life I have had! Everything happens to me."

True to her words, the law of attraction had consistently produced more and more hard times for her to face, in the form of ill health, family problems, indebtedness, and sheer poverty.

When this woman eventually learned of the law of attraction, she was living from day to day, wondering how she would meet the rent and struggling to provide food and clothing for her teen-age children, whom she had difficulty keeping in school and out of trouble. In addition, she had painful health problems for which there seemed no cure. Everything was wrong in her life, and she let the world know about it.

As she began to study the prosperity law of attraction, she realized that she had become a martyr to her problems and had dramatized them. She tried to reverse her thoughts and her words. She began to praise and bless every sign of improvement in her health, in her children, in her job, and in her financial affairs. She realized that she could not force her good, but she invited it. We invite the good by dwelling on the good.

As she constantly dwelt on the good, she reversed what she was attracting in her life. A better job was offered her; one of her children entered the armed forces and began sending home a monthly allotment check. The other children began to improve in their attitudes, behavior, and school work. One child got a part-time job after school which helped to provide him with clothes and spending money.

As the woman's attitude improved, so did her health. Then one day she received a letter from an attorney in her home state telling her that a relative had passed away, leaving her an entire estate: a house, a car, antique furniture, a mink coat, valuable jewelry, and stocks. She sold the house and acquired her other valuable inherited assets.

When we change what we think, we change what we attract. Although we cannot force good into our life, we can invite it by dwelling on it. When we do this, our good appears sometimes in amazing ways.

LIKE ATTRACTS LIKE

Emmet Fox has written in his booklet *Life Is Consciousness:*[2]

> If you came to me and told me that you can't get along with people, I should tell you to get a card about the size of a postcard, and write this on it: *"Like attracts like."* . . . People come to me and say, "If you only knew the kind of people I have to be with and work with!" I say, "The law of Being says, Like attracts like."

Most people with problems tend to concentrate on them, then wonder why they continue to have them. Begin to dwell on good and you will attract good things into your life. Good things will come your way consistently, without laborious effort, when you learn to expect them.

Dwell daily on some Truth writing, idea, or affirmation that uplifts you. Invite the good into your life. Do not spend your time merely hoping and wishing that everything will work out. Be willing to take some outer action to help work it out. That is what Joshua did. He did not merely hope that the Hebrews would

2. Available from Unity School of Christianity, Unity Village, Mo., 64065.

make it into the Promised Land, nor did he waste time fretting over their wilderness experiences. Instead, he frequently visited a high hill, deliberately studied the Promised Land, and definitely planned how he would enter it at the right time. When the right moment for action finally came, he was fully prepared for it, and took action unhesitatingly. All that he had planned on for forty years came to pass in just three days!

You can begin to invoke the prosperity law of mental attraction in a positive way by daily dwelling on these following decrees:

"I withdraw my strong thoughts and feelings from negation in every form. I do not dwell on negation. I do not try to explain it. I let it go and begin again with the good.

"The law of mental attraction now opens wide every rich channel of supply. I invite the powerful, loving action of God into my life, and every need is met. I expect the best and I now attract the best in every experience."

THE PROSPERITY LAW OF MENTAL ACCEPTANCE

— Chapter 4 —

Psychologists tell us that we can have anything that we can accept mentally; but if we cannot accept it mentally, we cannot get it — no matter what we do.

When people first learn that the power of thought is a means of attaining greater good in life, they sometimes try to rush into a demonstration that they have not mentally accepted. Their efforts meet only with defeat — and rightly so. Even when they demonstrate their desires temporarily, they cannot maintain the demonstration, because they have not developed a mental acceptance of the desired good. Their apparent demonstration ends in failure.

Writing on how to develop the law of mental acceptance, Mary L. Kupferle says, in *God Never Fails:*[1]

> All that we desire, all that we can ever envision or hope to attain is already provided for us; it is already available and will ever be awaiting our acceptance. . . . Most of us want to be good givers. We are eager to share all the fine and lovely things of life with others, but we sometimes forget that we must take the time and thought for receiving. Being a good receiver is not a complicated task, but a matter of simple application. As one Truth student puts it: "Take time, every day, quietly to let God give to you. Be still, sit quiet, and simply say to the loving Father, *'I am ready to receive, dear Father. I am ready to receive all the good You wish to give to me. I am receiving, now.'* "

MENTAL ACCEPTANCE AND THE PROMISED LAND

There is nothing new about the prosperity law of mental acceptance. In the Book of Numbers, we find the formula for it:

---

1. Mary L. Kupferle, *God Never Fails,*
(Unity Village, Mo: Unity Books, 1958).

The Lord commanded Moses to send twelve spies into the Promised Land to investigate the situation there. They were told to find out all they could about the Promised Land: whether the people were weak or strong; whether they were few or many; whether the land was fat or lean. (Numbers 13:17-20)

Of course, the Lord had already stated that the land was rich, flowing with milk and honey. He had been promising the Hebrews this fertile Promised Land for a long time. The spies were sent in for a psychological reason: to help them to accept mentally this fine Promised Land; to let them see at first hand the great blessings that awaited them there.

The twelve spies stayed there for forty days. In fact, they stayed so long that the Hebrews began to worry about them. When they returned, they gave conflicting reports. Joshua and Caleb were very excited about all that they had found. Caleb said, enthusiastically, "Let us go up at once, and occupy it; for we are well able to overcome it." They described it as rich, and brought back figs, pomegranates, and a cluster of grapes so big that it had to be carried on a staff by two men. This abundance of fruit was their proof that rich blessings awaited the Hebrews.

But, alas, Joshua and Caleb were the only "prosperous thinkers" among the twelve. The other ten spies gave an entirely different report: they stated that the land across the river was an evil land filled with giants, walled cities, and enemy forces.

Joshua tried to correct their false report: "The land, which we passed through . . . is an exceedingly good land. If the Lord delights in us, he will bring us into this land and give it to us, a land which flows with milk and honey." (Numbers 14:7,8)

As for the hostile forces in the land, he said: "Do not rebel against the Lord; and do not fear the people of the land; . . . their protection is removed from them, and the Lord is with us; do not fear them." (Numbers 14:9)

But the people had not listened. They had murmured and complained: "Would that we had died in the land of Egypt! . . . Our wives and our little ones will become a prey; . . . Let us go back to Egypt."

Historians state that the Hebrews sat and wept all night over their plight, even though their rich Promised Land was in plain view, awaiting them across the River Jordan!

What an example of people rejecting their good! With one bold stroke the Hebrews could have been in their Promised Land, but they rejected it and actually wanted to return to Egyptian bondage.

Psychologists say that when you think you

have been rejected, you have subconsciously rejected something. Your good *never* rejects you.

Jehovah had proved to the Hebrews time and time again that He wanted them to enter the Promised Land. He used signs and wonders to get them out of the clutches of Pharaoh, across the Red Sea, and safely through the wilderness: Yet they still doubted and feared.

At this point Jehovah realized that many of the Hebrews would never accept the idea of the Promised Land. They were still holding on to the past; to something that could never exist for them again; to something that had held no satisfaction for them. They had not yet learned the great truth that one cannot go back, one has to go forward; there is nothing to go back to.

Then Jehovah did what seemed a harsh thing, yet was actually the working of impersonal divine law: He decreed that all of those who had murmured against Him and against Moses would die in the wilderness.

This was the law of mental acceptance at work: Those who could not accept their Promised Land mentally would never get into it. Jehovah further declared that the Hebrews would remain in the wilderness until all the doubters and complainers had passed on.

WHY SOME DEMONSTRATE TRUTH
AND OTHERS DO NOT

This explains why some people demonstrate Truth and some do not. Those who get results are those who have released the past and have accepted mentally the possibility of new good. Those who hang on to the past, reject their good, and reject God's help in trying to give it to them, never do get the good they seek.

Perhaps you have heard someone say, "I have been studying Truth for twenty years, but still I cannot demonstrate health." A check on that person's attitudes will reveal that he is rejecting his good. He is still holding on to someone or something emotionally that he needs to release; health is not rejecting him, he is rejecting it.

THE FORMULA FOR ACCEPTING YOUR
GOOD: RELEASE THE PAST

What is the formula? How does one mentally accept his good?

First: Release the past.

Can you do it? If you have a long-unanswered prayer, a delayed healing, a dream that has not come true, remember that answered prayer, immediate healing, and realized dreams are not rejecting you. You are rejecting them!

Are you so attached to old patterns of living that you cannot get along comfortably without them? Are you emotionally attached to lack and illness?

If you truly want prosperity, do you still gain satisfaction from self-pity over your financial problems? You must give up something to make way for prosperity—probably self-pity and bitterness; probably the belief that you have had a hard time.

If you want a healing, you must be willing to give up the emotional satisfaction, sympathy, and attention that you get from being sick. A woman had been ill for some time; then she began to be healed spiritually. But as she did, she no longer got the attention and sympathy that had accompanied her illness. People began to say, "How well you look!" One day, unable to stand it any longer when a friend made this statement, she retorted, "I am not as well as you think!" And she went back to bed.

Jesus sometimes asked of those seeking healing: "Do you want to be healed?" God can only do for you what He can first do *through your mental attitudes*. Life demands much of the healthy person. He is expected to meet his share of life's responsibilities nonresistantly, even successfully. Physicians know that much that passes for illness is a subconscious attempt to escape life's responsibilities.

I recall as a child often accompanying my mother when she visited a neighbor who was always in bed in a dimly lit room, surrounded by medicine bottles. My mother always spoke in low tones to this woman who, in turn, described in vivid detail all her aches and pains. A devoted husband waited on her night and day.

Finally, after years of faithfully nursing his wife, this man passed away. Since there was no one else available to lavish attention and sympathy upon her, she arose from her sick bed and soon was going everywhere, visiting relatives and friends. Though for years she had been "bedridden," she never had another sick day.

Your good has not rejected you, but you may have rejected it by holding on to someone or something of the past or present. You may be holding on because of resentment, hate, unforgiveness, criticism, or emotional attachment. As was the case with the Hebrews of old, that which you complain about keeps you out of your promised land; that which you possessively hold on to keeps you out of your promised land. If you continue to hold on to it, you will never realize the greater health, wealth, and happiness that is your divine right.

Dare to let go of and forgive the past. Stop saying that you have had a hard time in life. Stop talking about unhappy experiences. Stop trying to get sympathy. As long as you do this, you are still emotionally attached to that hard experience; you are continuing to feed it emotionally; you are keeping it alive. There is no room in your thoughts and feelings for a better experience.

When we have reached the point where we take only the good in each experience and let the rest go, how swift and joyous will be our progress toward the realization of a happy, harmonious life.

Begin right now to say to yourself: *"I take only the good from each experience, past and present. I let the rest go."*

THINK OF YOUR LIFE AS YOU WANT IT TO BE

Second: Start thinking about your life the way you want it to be.

The way to accept mentally your promised land is simply to change your point of view. Recognize another set of circumstances or events as possible; then dwell upon that possibility.

Caleb recognized another set of circumstances as possible when he urged, "Let us go up at once, and occupy it; for we are well able to overcome it." (Numbers 13:30)

Joshua and Caleb recognized another set of circumstances as possible when they said to the complainers: "The land, which we passed through . . . is an exceedingly good land. If the Lord delights in us, he will bring us into this land and give it to us, a land which flows with milk and honey." (Numbers 14:7,8) Please note that Joshua and Caleb did not claim they could take the Promised Land alone. They claimed God's help.

Right there in the wilderness, Joshua refused to be hypnotized by some of the appearances of the Promised Land, such as walled cities and hostile forces. Instead, he dared to realize that another set of events and circumstances was possible in spite of appearances. He then began to decree them, claiming God's help in making them possible. He used the law of mental acceptance.

There once was a young man, the son of a poor farmer, who began to study Truth. Because he had had no training and believed he had little ability, he had no confidence in himself. He had always said: "I never had a chance. Life has been hard on me. I'm just a poor nobody."

But as he began to study Truth, he realized that he was a spiritual being, a somebody, entitled to all the opportunities, privileges, and blessings that his loving Father had for him.

Instead of making further excuses for his failure in life he started affirming: *"Lord, I am ready!"* He began to accept mentally his promised land, by recognizing another set of circumstances was possible, and by asking God's help in manifesting them.

Then a wonderful thing happened: He was given a scholarship to a leading university, where he became a full-time student well on the way to a happy, prosperous life.

But this did not happen until he stopped talking about his hard life and bemoaning his lack of opportunity.

GET READY TO ACCEPT YOUR GOOD

Begin now to recognize that another set of circumstances and events is possible in your own life. Then ask God's help, and affirm often, *"Lord, I am ready!"* If you really are ready, mentally and emotionally, to accept greater good, it will come very soon. And once it starts, you cannot stop it; you have to flow along with it. So be sure you mean it when you say, *"Lord, I am ready."*

As one Truth student has said, "I have never yet seen a case of unanswered prayer, when the one who prayed was really ready to receive the answer." In my own life, I have always got what I prayed for just as soon as I could accept it mentally. Furthermore, I always receive my answer at the level of my acceptance — no more, no less.

After Joshua had seen the Promised Land, he had to wait forty years before going into it. He had to wait for the doubters and complainers to pass on in the wilderness.

During this long period, Joshua might have fretted because of the delay that was being caused by others. But Joshua realized that he needed this delay. He turned it into a blessing. He actually needed this period as a time for preparing and planning.

He was a master planner. During those forty years, he quietly planned how he would take the Promised Land. Often he would go up on Mount Nebo and from that high point quietly study the land, planning how to get into it, and how to possess it once he was in it. One day, all that he had accepted mentally and planned for happened. After a forty-year wait, the Hebrews went into the Promised Land in just three days!

It is wise to keep quiet about your plans, your desires, and the good you want in life. Be like Joshua: refrain from blaming others for apparent delays. Go up in consciousness on Mount Nebo, and there study your situation objectively, as you keep picturing the good you want. (The word *Nebo* means "height." Metaphysically it means "foresight.") Realize that the delay is good, because it is a time of preparation. When you have accepted your good mentally, it will quickly appear. Suddenly it will all be done, and with one bold stroke you will find yourself in your promised land.

Realization precedes manifestation. A realization of Truth will banish every ill, and the prayer through which realization comes is the prayer that asserts the truth. Joshua proved this—and so can you.

The following statements can help you gain a realization of Truth that will help you to accept and then possess your promised land:

"I take only the good from each experience. I let the rest go."

"I begin now to recognize another set of circumstances as possible. I am not hypnotized by appearances."

"My progress is swift and joyous. I am living a happy, harmonious life now."

"Lord, I am ready! I mentally accept and claim my highest good now."